Fairy Tale Creatures

Goblins

by Emma Huddleston

Fitchburg Public Library
5530 Lacy Road
Fitchburg, WI 53711

FOCUS READERS.
BEACON

www.focusreaders.com

Copyright © 2022 by Focus Readers®, Lake Elmo, MN 55042. All rights reserved. No part of this book may be reproduced or utilized in any form or by any means without written permission from the publisher.

Focus Readers is distributed by North Star Editions:
sales@northstareditions.com | 888-417-0195

Produced for Focus Readers by Red Line Editorial.

Photographs ©: Shutterstock Images, cover, 1, 4, 6, 8, 11, 14–15, 21, 22, 25, 26, 29; iStockphoto, 13, 16, 18

Library of Congress Cataloging-in-Publication Data
Names: Huddleston, Emma, author.
Title: Goblins : fairy tale creatures / by Emma Huddleston.
Description: Lake Elmo, MN : Focus Readers, [2022] | Series: Fairy tale creatures | Includes index. | Audience: Grades 2-3
Identifiers: LCCN 2021010631 (print) | LCCN 2021010632 (ebook) | ISBN 9781637390054 (hardcover) | ISBN 9781637390122 (paperback) | ISBN 9781637390191 (ebook) | ISBN 9781637390252 (pdf)
Subjects: LCSH: Goblins--Juvenile literature.
Classification: LCC GR549 .H84 2022 (print) | LCC GR549 (ebook) | DDC 398.24/54--dc23
LC record available at https://lccn.loc.gov/2021010631
LC ebook record available at https://lccn.loc.gov/2021010632

Printed in the United States of America
Mankato, MN
082021

About the Author

Emma Huddleston lives in Minnesota with her husband. She enjoys writing children's books and spending time outside. She also likes reading fairy tales and mysteries.

Table of Contents

CHAPTER 1
Sneaky Spirit 5

CHAPTER 2
All Kinds of Goblins 9

STORY SPOTLIGHT
Greedy Goblins 14

CHAPTER 3
Looks and Powers 17

CHAPTER 4
Help or Harm 23

Focus on Goblins • 28
Glossary • 30
To Learn More • 31
Index • 32

Chapter 1

Sneaky Spirit

A man walked through the forest alone. It was a moonless night. The sky was very dark. If he wasn't careful, he could get lost.

Suddenly, the man saw a light in the distance. It seemed to move.

 Goblins are known for their creepy looks and tricky behavior.

 Several legends tell of creatures that get people lost in marshes or bogs.

He tried to walk toward the light. But it kept moving away. The man followed the light as it flashed and danced. At last, he got close enough to see what it was. The light came from a candle. A small creature held it. The creature was a goblin!

The goblin led the man to a cliff. Then it winked at him and blew the candle out. The man was left in the dark.

Sometimes a group of goblins dance together. The dance makes people fall asleep.

Chapter 2

All Kinds of Goblins

Goblins appear in stories from around the world. Some legends are very old. They tell of sneaky spirits. But the creatures are not always bad. For example, dokkaebi appear in many Korean **folktales**.

 Buildings in ancient Korea often had pictures of dokkaebi on their roof tiles.

Some of these stories are more than 1,000 years old. Dokkaebi often want to meet people or play games. But they can also cause disease or start fires.

In Japan, people told legends of the tengu. These spirits live in mountains. They have wings

Dokkaebi have power over sea creatures. Sometimes they help people catch fish.

 Some tengu have beaks and claws like birds.

like birds. They also have long beaks or large noses.

In early stories, tengu were evil. They kidnapped children. Later, the stories became funnier and less scary.

Mischievous spirits also appear in folktales from North America. The legends vary depending on the **Indigenous** nation. Each group has its own stories.

Algonquin legends tell of small people who live in the forest. These beings are usually not dangerous. But in Wampanoag legends, the creatures can hurt or kidnap people.

In Europe, goblin stories were told as early as the 1300s. Many stories spread throughout England,

 Kobolds appear in German folktales. These goblin-like creatures help in people's homes.

Ireland, and Wales. Others came from Denmark or Germany. Goblins in these **Western** legends were more likely to behave badly. Some spirits were just naughty. Others were said to be evil. But all used magic to play tricks.

STORY SPOTLIGHT

Greedy Goblins

Goblins appear in many popular books and movies. One example is the Harry Potter **series**. In these stories, goblins run a large bank. Hundreds of goblins work there. They guard money and treasure. They keep it locked in **vaults** that are deep underground.

The goblins are very smart. But they also tend to be greedy and mean. As a result, they sometimes get into fights.

Besides banking, some goblins work as silversmiths. They make swords, jewelry, and armor. Goblins are very proud of these beautiful objects.

Goblins in the Harry Potter series have pointed ears.

Chapter 3

Looks and Powers

A goblin's appearance can vary depending on the story. Tengu have wings. Dokkaebi have long teeth and claws. Sometimes they have horns, too.

 Depending on the story, goblins may also be called hobgoblins or bugbears.

17

 People in Europe told stories of many small, strange-looking creatures.

In stories from Europe, goblins are often similar to fairies. In fact, people sometimes used the terms **interchangeably**. For example, Welsh people told stories of fairies that lived underground. The Welsh called these creatures "coblynau."

This name sounds a little bit like the word *goblin*.

Many goblins have small bodies. They often look very ugly. Their ears and noses tend to be quite large. They may also have huge mouths and bulging eyes. A few goblins are covered in hair.

In one legend, a goblin lives in a castle. She can turn into ivy and grow on the walls.

Some goblins are **invisible**. These goblins are similar to ghosts. They can't be seen. But they can make sounds and throw things. These goblins often live in or near houses. But they sometimes live in swamps or forests. Stories warn travelers to watch out. Meeting a goblin could be very dangerous.

Fun Fact

Some goblins have the power to send people flying through the air.

 Some types of goblins can cast spells and do magic.

Many goblins have magical powers. Some can shape-shift. They can make themselves look like people or animals. Other goblins can **predict** when people will die. Goblins often use these powers to trick or scare people.

21

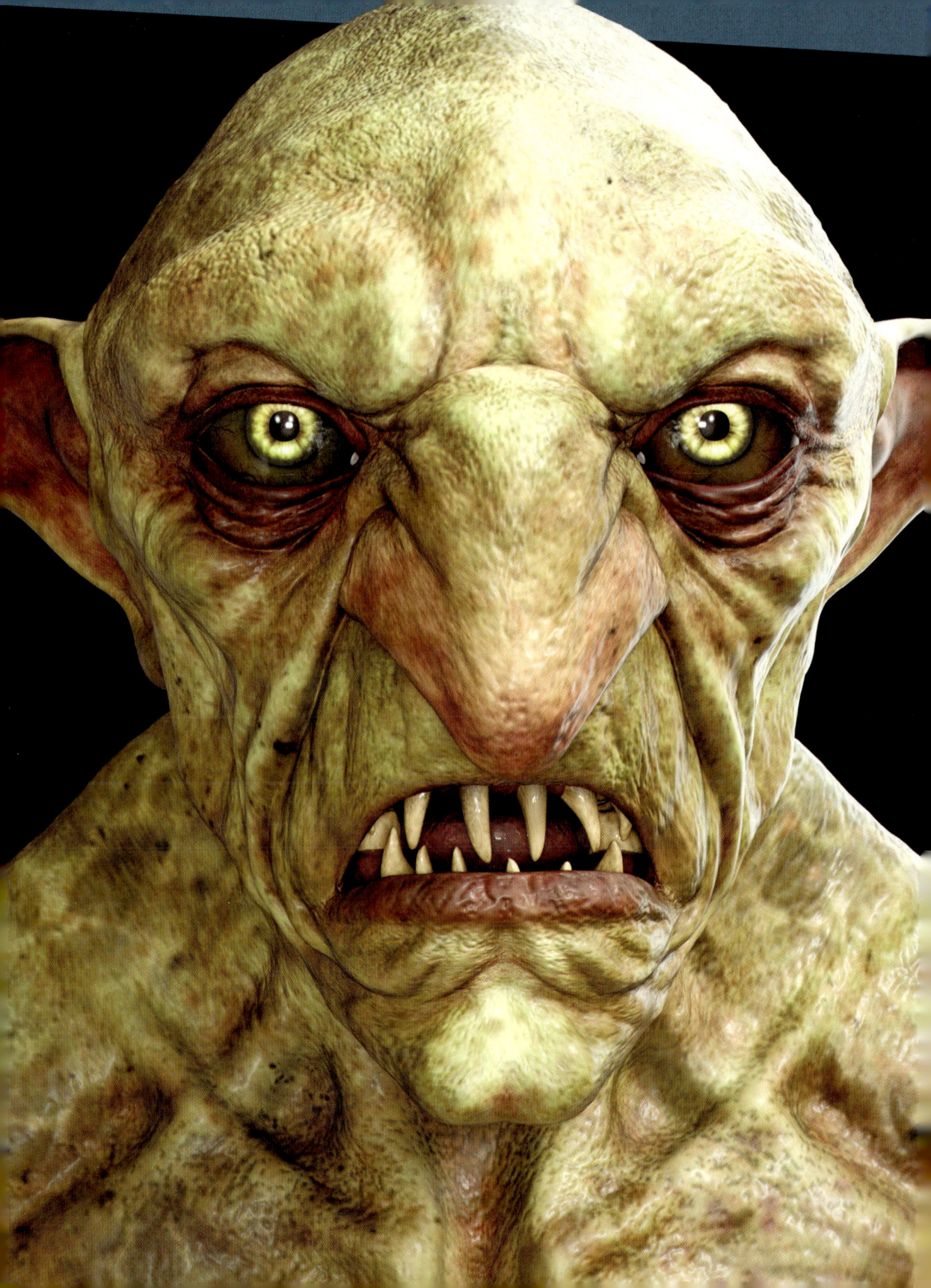

Chapter 4

Help or Harm

Goblins tend to be mischievous. They like to play pranks on people. These tricks confuse or annoy people. But they usually don't hurt anyone. For example, goblins may move people's furniture at night.

In many stories, goblins have bad tempers. They get angry easily.

23

They may also take or hide people's belongings. The people wake up to a surprise.

In many stories, goblins make loud noises. They try to scare or disturb people. Some goblins bang on pots and pans. Others screech and rattle windows or doors.

In a few stories, goblins are meaner. These goblins try to get people lost. They **lure** people deep into the woods or swamp. Some of those people never return. And a

 Legends of goblins might warn people to stay away from swamps and other dangerous places.

few goblins are said to hurt or kidnap people.

However, not all goblins are bad. Some will help people do chores.

 To get help from a goblin, people might set out bread or cream.

But first, people need to give them something. For example, people can give the goblins food. Or they can light a fire for heat. In return, the goblins may help care for their home or farm.

Other goblins help miners. Some knock on the rock to show miners good places to dig. Others warn miners of danger. If something bad is about to happen, the goblins tap the mine's wall three times. In fact, some stories even say goblins can be good luck.

Some goblins punish naughty children. But they bring gifts for children who behave well.

FOCUS ON
Goblins

Write your answers on a separate piece of paper.

1. Write a sentence describing the main ideas of Chapter 4.

2. Legends of goblins tend to be creepy. Do you enjoy reading scary stories? Why or why not?

3. Which creatures appear in Korean folktales?
    A. dokkaebi
    B. tengu
    C. coblynau

4. What do goblins and fairies have in common?
    A. Neither creature can do magic.
    B. Both creatures always have wings.
    C. Both creatures often have small bodies.

5. What does **behave** mean in this book?

Some goblins punish naughty children. But they bring gifts for children who behave well.

    A. to act in a certain way
    B. to do bad or rude things
    C. to turn into frogs

6. What does **disturb** mean in this book?

In many stories, goblins make loud noises. They try to scare or disturb people.

    A. to bother someone
    B. to make someone happy
    C. to make someone feel safe

Answer key on page 32.

Glossary

folktales
Stories that have been told out loud for many years.

Indigenous
Having ancestors who lived in a region before colonists arrived.

interchangeably
In place of one another, often because they are similar.

invisible
Not able to be seen.

lure
To convince someone to come near.

mischievous
Liking to cause trouble.

predict
To tell what will happen in the future.

series
A set of books, movies, or stories about the same characters.

vaults
Rooms that are designed to safely store money and other valuable items.

Western
Coming from or shaped by the people and ideas of Europe and North America.

To Learn More

BOOKS

Abdo, Kenny. *Ghosts*. Minneapolis: Abdo Publishing, 2020.

Gagliardi, Sue. *Fairies*. Lake Elmo, MN: Focus Readers, 2019.

Sautter, A. J. *Discover Orcs, Boggarts, and Other Nasty Fantasy Creatures*. Mankato, MN: Capstone Press, 2018.

NOTE TO EDUCATORS

Visit **www.focusreaders.com** to find lesson plans, activities, links, and other resources related to this title.

Index

A
Algonquin, 12

C
coblynau, 18

D
dokkaebi, 9–10, 17

E
evil, 11, 13

F
folktales, 9, 12
forests, 5, 12, 20

H
Harry Potter, 14

J
Japan, 10

K
Korean, 9

N
noises, 24

P
powers, 10, 20–21

T
tengu, 10–11, 17
tricks, 13, 21, 23

W
Wampanoag, 12
Western, 13

Answer Key: 1. Answers will vary; **2.** Answers will vary; **3.** A; **4.** C; **5.** A; **6.** A